# Color Me in SUNFLOWERS

**BY JODIE BEAU**

© 2020

 @colorme.bad

# BE BOLD.

HOLD
YOUR HEAD
high

faith.

Another
day of
sun

homegrown

beautiful.
fierce. free.

L VE

Be
the
light

A flower doesn't compete with the flowers next to it.

It just blooms.

Love
me.
But leave
me
WILD

let it be

Summer

# STAND TALL

IF YOU
CAN'T SEE
THE
sunshine
BE THE
sunshine

Grow
through
what you go
through

love by the Moon, live by the Sun

PEACE ☮ LOVE ♥ SUNFLOWERS

SPREAD SEEDS OF
happiness

Wild
CHILD

I got those sunshine vibes

Bloom
where you are planted

Plant
flowers.

Grow
laughter.

Harvest
love.

Let there be peace
on Earth

sunshine
-AND-
whiskey

Wild & free.

# Wonderfully chaotic.

## A PERFECTLY BEAUTIFUL MESS

# ALL FLOWERS GROW THROUGH DIRT.